Heresy in the Making

Hera C Weaver

Heresy in the Making © 2023 Hera C Weaver

All rights reserved.

No part of this publication may be reproduced, stored in a retrieval system, or transmitted, in any form or by any means, electronic, mechanical, photocopying, recording or otherwise, without the prior written permission of the presenters.

Hera C Weaver asserts the moral right to be identified as author of this work.

Presentation by *BookLeaf Publishing*

Web: www.bookleafpub.com

E-mail: info@bookleafpub.com

ISBN: 9789357696722

First edition 2023

DEDICATION

This book is dedicated to my Inner Child,

I can't change the past and I can no longer live in it. I can, however, rewrite the stories that fostered negative Self and World views and beliefs by assigning a different meaning to the experiences of the past, a meaning that repurposes our story to allow the lessons learned from our challenges to become our greatest gifts. To rewrite a story, we must first document the original story….let's begin

ACKNOWLEDGEMENT

I've heard that in life, you may have multiple teachers who aid in guiding you onto your intended path, some knowingly and purposefully, others unexpectedly and without their own awareness, in either case, I've been fortunate enough to have many teachers impart their knowledge, wisdom, and compassion on me.

So to all the teachers I have encountered, Thank You for showing up for me and for caring for me in ways that I was unable to care for myself, I promise to pay it forward.

PREFACE

“As traumatised children, we always dreamed that someone would come and save us. We never dreamed that it would, in fact, be ourselves, as adults.”

-Alice Little

Loss of Innocence

Back then, the emotions that I felt, I couldn't fully
comprehend, let alone name

As the years passed, I discovered that they're called
inferiority, rejection, fear & shame

Gathering my courage, I tried to give voice to the
trauma and pain

My adolescent mind working overtime attempting to
verbalize adult concepts in vain

Endeavors to deflect by Caregivers focused on
invalidating my experience caused a shift in my brain

From this point forward, I would never be the same

Fragments of Me

Stripped of everything including my autonomy,
I'm not safe here and neither is my femininity

Feeling helpless as a child turned my I's to We,
no longer whole, using plurals to reference the
fractures internally

Struggling to survive an environment of apathy
from those meant to care for us unconditionally

My Caregivers no longer concealed their
malignity, their contempt now apparent and
focused on us intently

An absence of support perpetuated an
unsureness of self that haunted us incessantly

The reality of our family dynamics spawned the
bitterness of betrayal and stoked the flames of
our resentment angrily & relentlessly

Void of a voice, we excelled in literature
unexpectedly, using the pen as a sword, striking
our target with flair and accuracy

Loss of Inheritance

It was once said that the ones to inherit the Earth will be the meek

On the verge of a cataclysmic breakdown, I brace myself, knowing this means my future is destined to be bleak

Incensed by the lack of familial concern, my heart hardened as the maltreatment reached my peak

Unconcerned with the forfeiture of the inheritance because it's my Caregiver's atonement I seek

Underwhelming Guidance Counseling

Those that would benefit from my ignorance
reinforce false realities over my truth citing my
over-active imagination

Frustration elevates to rage and has me lashing out
resulting in being told to find healthier ways of
communication

Unmotivated to participate in any adolescent
conversations, focused on escaping my hell which
only adds to my sense of alienation

Feeling disempowered has me spinning my wheels in
an unknowingly vicious cycle that leads to loss of
agency caused by my own disidentification

Epidemic of Epigenetic

Parents born of parents unable to support the
development of the generation they've birthed

Creating destructive cycles in attempts to self-soothe
from the hurt

Leaving shadows lurking just beneath the surface
waiting to be unearthed

Unaware of the familial pattern, hyper-focused on
self, feeling alone and cursed

Rebelling against the injustice, belligerent behavior
queued and ready to assert

Defenses up, finger-pointing, and victim-blaming
clash with the objectives of reflection & attunement,
rendering both inert

Emotional Inheritance

The truth is that traumatic experiences shape and
change the capabilities of the brain

Toxic thought patterns modeled before me,
solidifying irrational and unregulated emotional &
mental terrain

My observations of the toxic thought patterns reveal
itself as a legacy of trauma, the depths of which are
so deep that I struggle to ascertain

Fear of uncertainty activated survival mechanisms
and mental defenses to aid in predicting the thoughts
of others, in hopes of avoiding further pain

The thing about emotionally immature parenting is
that it's unpredictable, making pain-avoidant efforts
to predict mostly in vain

Its Morphin' Time

Those seeking power over me think that my young age will make it easy to deceive

But persevering trauma has sharpened my survival instincts in ways that they cannot know or perceive

With my survival mind on high alert, I can see thru the manipulative plans they've conceived

Queening the Pawn in this game of psychological warfare and claiming my space on the board with ease

Trapped By Trauma

Unconsciously allowing the pain of the past to dictate
my present & future path

Feeling unsafe in the World, shrouded in shadows &
emotionally detached

Distrustful of the intentions of others, guarded and
ready to unleash my wrath

Emotions dysregulated and behaviors equally &
erratically matched

Remorse consumes me as I am met with my
consequences in the aftermath

Consumer Religion

Preoccupied with finding my value in the money that
I have to spend

Everyone seems so content, so I'm doing my best to
blend

Hiding uncomfortable feelings on the inside,
conditioned to play pretend

Seeking external gratification, now I'm caught in a
consuming trend

Widely accepted to shop for less but spend more
money than we intend

In the aftermath, what felt good in the moment was
quick to spiral and descend

Consumerism is a tool of distraction we have yet to
fully realize and comprehend

Dark Night of the Soul

Restless nights with darkness stretching on without an end in sight

Dreams turn to nightmares as my fears resurface and take flight

Traumatic memories mingle with fear causing my anxiety to soar to new heights

Tendrils of smoke spiraled slowly suffocating me while snuffing out my light

Scenes of my life flicker and fade out as my vision succumbs to the darkness of night

I find myself at a crossroads wondering which path to take, the light of the left or the darkness of the right

Within the Darkness

Consciously and Cautiously, I travel deeper into the
darkness

Ahead, there's light in the distance, enough for me to
view my surroundings in all of its starkness

The shadows shift and swirl with muffled incoherent
whispers and sporadic sharpness

My heart in my throat, I continue forward as they
begin to circle me overhead like vultures to a carcass

They torpedo to me and thru me, striking with a
frightening but tolerable harshness

Images of ancestors known & unknown flash in an
unfamiliar synthesis, leaving me raw and feeling
every bit of my emotional catharsis

Mystery Machine

Living in trauma, I was always guarded, looking for a fight, ready to be tested, so I was Super Scrappy

I spoke without regard to the feelings of others which was sometimes funny but oftentimes just tacky

I found myself thinking that everyone was out to get me which had me living in my superiority but feeling overall crappy

When I would attempt to assess why I was feeling that way, I couldn't quite solve that mystery, I just knew that I wasn't happy

Lessons Learned

I read once that we create what's called a soul
contract before we incarnate here

I choose to believe it because to me, it makes the
purpose of my experiences clear

I've learned that for every action, an equal and
opposite reaction will appear

So I'm keeping my focus on developing Self instead
of my anxiety & fear

With the intent to be free of Karma, to the
Holographic Universal Laws, I will adhere

Number 5 is Alive

Waking up in a World with electric thoughts and magnetic feelings

Short-circuiting my way to deep realizations and profound healing

Euphorically experiencing relationships where engagement is aimed at mutually beneficial dealings

Focused on my inner work, no longer prioritizing the breaking of glass ceilings

Spellbound

Pointing the finger, I find that blame is binding, as I bind so am I bound

Truths hidden in plain sight, taking note of my findings, as I seek so am I found

Opting for open-hearted connections in spite of the pain, As I love, so will it surround

Breathing life into bonds, transmuting energy with my words, As I speak so will it resound

Releasing the past, living there feels restrictive and confining, As I pray, its for peace profound

Truly, Truly, Truly Outrageous

I'm removing the binds of society's expectations and challenging the status quo

Putting action to my dreams and mapping out the places I intend to go

I'm planting seeds of hope and watching my confidence bloom and grow

Leaving in the past my pain & suffering of long ago

This is only the beginning, I have way more to sow

Bet you can't believe your eyes oh whoa

New Phone, Who Dis

Surrendering to my Higher Self, balancing emotional needs, logical reasoning, and intuition

Realizing, it's just Me, Myself & I, a.k.a, Mind, Body, and Soul, in this spiritual coalition

We're more alike than we are different but simultaneously incomparable so there is no competition

Newfound awareness rebuilds positive beliefs giving credence to my dreams and premonitions

Feeling self-content in the reality that I'm choosing to experience, me and my emotions, and actions are no longer in opposition

I AM

I am prioritizing emotional clarity over awareness as part of my human design

I am moving in connection with my inner authority and paying attention to the signs

I am making need-based improvements in my life, one implementation at a time

I am recognizing myself as partly imperfect and wholly energetically divine.

www.ingramcontent.com/pod-product-compliance
Lightning Source LLC
LaVergne TN
LVHW012155060726
842759LV00028B/847

* 9 7 8 9 3 5 7 6 9 6 7 2 2 *